The Puppeteer

S. D. JONES

GLOBE FEARON
Pearson Learning Group

DOUBLE FASTBACK® SPY BOOKS

Against the Wall
The Black Gold Conspiracy
Claw the Cold, Cold Earth
A Dangerous Game
Escape From East Berlin
The Last Red Rose
Picture of Evil
The Puppeteer
The Race to Ross
The Silver Spy

All photography © Pearson Education, Inc. (PEI) unless specifically noted.

Copyright © 2004 by Pearson Education, Inc., publishing as Globe Fearon®, an imprint of Pearson Learning Group, 299 Jefferson Road, Parsippany, NJ 07054. All rights reserved. No part of this book may be reproduced or transmitted in any form or by any means, electronic or mechanical, including photocopying, recording, or by any information storage and retrieval system, without permission in writing from the publisher. For information regarding permission(s), write to Rights and Permissions Department.

Globe Fearon® and Fastback® are registered trademarks of Globe Fearon, Inc.

ISBN 0-13-024626-3
Printed in the United States of America
1 2 3 4 5 6 7 8 9 10   07 06 05 04 03

1-800-321-3106
www.pearsonlearning.com

The man in the shadows was 50 feet away. Porter could just make out his form. He was probably more than 6 feet tall, but the giant columns of the Lincoln Memorial made him look small. He was bent over in the cold, collar up, hat pulled low over his brow.

This was the man Porter knew only as "the Puppeteer." The man had cheated his country for years. He gave—or sold—secrets to the KGB, the intelligence service of the enemy side in the years of tension between East and West. Porter had waited long for this moment. This meeting with him had been secretly arranged. Now at last, Porter was about to learn the identity of the CIA's most wanted double agent.

Porter pulled his gloves tight against his fingers. He felt for his gun and made his way toward the man. The cold white moon threw a blue light onto the Lincoln Memorial. That made it look as though it had been carved out of a single chunk of ice. Porter made his way carefully over the slippery steps.

The man in the shadows moved, just slightly, to his left. It was only a little move. But it gave Porter a chill. He stopped in his tracks, eyes wide, straining to see what had caught the Puppeteer's attention.

The man moved again. This time he moved quickly, jerking his body around, looking surprised. Porter raced up the stairs and threw his body against a column. He pulled out his gun. For a moment, he lost sight of the Puppeteer. Then he took two steps to the right and found him again. This time the man was running down the steps. He tripped, but regained his balance quickly. What was he running from? Porter had left strict instructions for Wes Tyson to keep his men out of this operation.

Then Porter saw the second figure—another shadow, a smaller frame. This figure wore a hat and coat. But a tuft of long, wild hair gave away the sex. It was a woman. She had a gun. Porter followed the Puppeteer, putting himself between the man and the woman.

Porter tried his best to keep an eye on both of them. He turned around in time to see the woman take aim.

The Puppeteer turned and cried out, "Marta, no!" in a high-pitched, panicked scream.

She fired. Both men dropped safely to the ground. She had missed her target. The bullet hit a lamppost. Who was she firing at?

Porter would have returned fire if he hadn't heard that name. "Marta." He had heard it before. Many times. He had also spoken it before, in tender whispers. "Marta."

He scrambled to his feet and saw the woman run to a waiting car. It rumbled from the shadows, stopped only to pick her up, then disappeared into the night. Porter had turned his gaze from the Puppeteer for no more than a few seconds. But when he looked up again, the man was gone. Porter was suddenly alone, in the quiet night. But the name "Marta" was still running through his brain. "Marta . . . Marta . . ."

J. K. Porter was jerked from his sleep by the sound of water splashing. He sat up so suddenly that he nearly tipped over his canoe. He shook the sleep from his head. Then he quickly reached for his gun. But what he pulled from his pocket was a flashlight.

By the time Porter figured out where he was and what he was doing, the fish had freed itself from the hook. It had swallowed the worm. In a show of fun, the fish flipped its tail just before diving down into the cool green waters of Seven Tree Lake.

"Next time no mercy," Porter yelled at the fish. He laughed and surprised himself.

He did not usually like watching his breakfast swim away—and it happened more than he cared to admit. But it had been a long time since he heard the sound of his own laughter. He liked it.

Porter brought his reel in and took up the paddle. Fish or no fish, he was hungry. Today he'd have eggs for breakfast.

"This was a good idea, James," he told himself and headed for the shore. It was at least the sixth time in two days he had congratulated himself for taking a well-earned vacation. August in Maine was his favorite time. Union, Maine, was his favorite little town. And Seven Tree Lake was the best place to fish.

Porter took great satisfaction in imagining what Wes Tyson and the boys were doing back in hot, sticky Washington,

D.C. There was no way of finding out, of course. He had taken a cabin with no phone, no radio, and no TV. His only link to the outside world was Alex, the postman, who stopped by daily. Washington, D.C. may as well have been on the moon.

When Porter reached shore, he relived the moment when his vacation began. He remembered the look on Wes Tyson's face when he dropped the 100-page report on his desk.

"Here's a little weekend reading for you," Porter had quipped, trying a little humor on for size. It didn't go over well. Tyson looked as though Porter had thrown him a live fish.

"Should I be pleased that I have to read through 100 pages of your lousy writing, only to uncover what we both already know? That you never *did* find out who the Puppeteer is! And there is still a double agent somewhere in the agency! Now I have to go back to my bosses, throw up my arms, and say, 'Gee, I'm sorry. We couldn't find him.'"

"You pulled me off the case," Porter answered defensively. "You closed the case."

"Because you and Carradine couldn't turn up a thing. But at least now the big boys will stop snooping around my department and look for the traitor in someone *else's* backyard."

Porter knew that deep down, Tyson was happy that his best agents had come up empty-handed. As for Porter, he was happy just to be finished with this rough case. Months had gone by since the meeting with the Puppeteer had fallen through. That icy night he had lost him forever. And lost Marta as well.

The "Old Man," as everyone called Tyson, lifted his white-haired head and glanced at Porter. "All right. Good job. But I want to see you *and* Carradine in my office first thing Monday morning. After I've had a chance to go through this—"

"Uh, about Monday," Porter had interrupted him. "I start vacation at six o'clock today."

As Porter took up his fishing tackle, he remembered the storm clouds brewing over Tyson's head when the Old Man heard the news.

"Yes, this was a good idea, James," Porter told himself again.

Back at the cabin, Porter made himself breakfast. He secretly missed having the fish, but he'd settle for the eggs.

Later, as he lingered over his third cup of coffee, he stepped onto the porch. He noticed that Alex, the postman, had already picked up the postcard that Porter had addressed to his sister. Alex always picked up the mail at night on his way back from his shift at the post office. Beyond the mailbox and across the dirt street were woods full of pines, birches, and a few elms. The elms were dying or already dead. Still, they stood proudly above the rest. Porter stretched and sighed, enjoying the peace and calm.

He was not ready for the shock. No one is ever ready to suddenly see someone he knows outside of his usual setting. So it was with the figure now walking up the dirt road. Not only was he out of his ordinary setting, but he wasn't wearing his usual blue suit either. He was dressed in blue jeans, a light cotton shirt, and a down vest. He was carrying a backpack. And the white hair on the man's head glowed in the sunlight.

"Oh, no," said Porter aloud. "It's the *Old Man!*"

Porter put down his coffee cup and came down off the porch. He tried to smile, but he knew it must have looked like a frown. He waved and wondered if Tyson could see how upset he was. He felt sick and weak in the knees. It was as though he had been caught doing something wrong. And this feeling was made worse by the look on the Old Man's face. It was bright and cheerful—as though he were pleased with himself. Pleased that he could still track a man down.

"Hello, Porter!" Tyson called. His voice sounded chipper. When Tyson was a few yards away he stopped and showed a silly grin. "Surprise," he said merrily.

That statement made Porter angry. In the minute that he had to prepare himself, he had practiced saying all sorts of nice things. But now all he could say was, "What are you doing here?"

Tyson laughed. "Is that any way for a man to treat his boss?"

"It is when the man was trying to forget his boss," Porter replied.

Tyson handed Porter his backpack and breathed a sigh of relief. "Whew. I don't mind telling you it's been a good while since I did any hiking. Of course I got a ride from Route 17. Is that cheating?"

Tyson dropped himself into one of the rockers that sat on the front porch. He took in the same view that Porter had admired just minutes ago.

"Anyone know you're here?" Porter asked.

"Nope." He looked over at Porter. "Pretty sneaky, eh?"

Porter pulled up another chair—a smaller one, with one leg shorter than the others. He noticed that Tyson had already muscled in and taken the best chair. He looked at the Old Man's smiling face. It was an empty face, the smile of an idiot. He was too happy. Something was wrong.

"Wes? Are you all right?" Porter asked.

"You bet. Be pretty hard for a man to be unhappy up here. Wouldn't you say?"

Porter nodded cautiously.

"Got any coffee?" Tyson asked.

Porter got him coffee.

Tyson drank the first half cup in total silence. He stared as though he were hypnotized by the sight and smell of the pines. Then he said, "I like Maine. Never been here before, but I like it."

"I like it too," Porter said. "It's quiet. You can be *all alone* up here."

"Funny. I always chose Florida for vacations," Tyson went on. "Don't know why. Habit, I guess. But this . . . this is . . . you can keep Miami Beach."

Porter finally said, "Wes, what are you doing here?"

Tyson pretended not to hear him. He stood and walked across the porch. His eyes followed the path of a hawk as it made a figure eight above a row of pine trees.

Porter said, "No offense, Wes, but I came up here to relax. I've been dreaming about that Puppeteer report every time I close my eyes. I need the rest."

Tyson did not answer right away. He was still watching the hawk. "Now that's freedom. A bird has true freedom. Do you know how long I've been with the agency? Since I was 30. That's 35 years. I've seen a lot of people come and go. I've seen young men killed, and old men waste away behind their desks. You get to ask some pretty big questions when you're my age. I've filed my last report, J. K. I'm retiring."

So that's what all this talk was about. The Old Man was going to retire. He was 65 years old, and he wanted to settle down. It was news that Porter certainly could have waited two weeks to hear.

Porter tried to act surprised. "I'm real happy for you, Wes. You've worked hard and you deserve a rest. But please don't tell me that you chose this cabin to retire to."

Finally Wes Tyson looked Porter squarely in the eyes. That made Porter breathe easier. This was the old Wes Tyson. He was back on planet earth again. He was glaring at Porter the way he always did.

"I want you to take my place," he said.

Porter was so startled, he didn't say a word. Then Tyson asked to see the lake. When they reached the lake's shore, a few moments later, Tyson picked up a small rock and threw it out in the water. Both men watched the stone make a high curved arch and then burst through the lake's surface.

"Why me?" Porter asked finally.

"You've got what it takes. You're old enough to be cautious, but not too old to take chances. I've always liked your work. You're the man I want."

"What about Carradine?" Porter asked. "He's your right-hand man. He knows almost as much about the department as you do."

"What about him? He'll be angry. He'll get over it. He'll have to."

"Well, I'm glad you like my work," Porter said.

"And I'm glad you're glad," Tyson said. "So what do you think?"

"I know I can do a good job. Better than Carradine, I think. But I also know that you didn't come all the way up here to tell me you were retiring, and that you want me to take your place."

Tyson looked at Porter, pleased with him for having figured things out. He said, "You and I have been together for 20 years. I've kind of looked at you as my prize student. I taught you everything I know. I trust you—"

"So what is it?" asked Porter.

Tyson looked him right between the eyes. "It's your report."

"What about it?"

"I read through it. We think that you've left out some important information. Things don't track. We think you're holding something back."

"We?"

"Carradine, me—"

"Of course, it *would* be Carradine."

"It shouldn't matter to you what he thinks. Others feel the same."

"This is great. You want me to take your place. But you don't trust me to put together a truthful report."

"I told you I trust you. That's why I didn't call you back. That's why I came out here—by myself. In the office things would have been handled formally. The top people are asking some pretty serious questions. And I'm the one who's going to have to answer them."

"They think *I'm* the double agent?" Porter asked.

Tyson just stood there, cool and calm. "You'd better tell me the whole story," he said. "If you do, I can set things right. It's time you laid your cards on the table, James."

The fire felt good. Even the summer evenings in Maine were cool, sometimes chilly. The fire helped warm the room. This room, this evening, needed warmth. Porter threw another log onto the fire. He shoved it in place. He watched the flames leap and hiss. Then he poured Wes Tyson a glass of sherry. Porter knew that Tyson always drank a glass after dinner. Porter poured himself another cup of coffee.

Now Tyson's presence in Union, Maine made sense. J. K. Porter was under suspicion. Tyson and his bosses saw something in the report that made them wonder about Porter. Porter was sure Carradine fueled the fire of their doubts. He and Carradine had never liked each other.

"Can I get you anything else?" Porter asked. He tried to keep the bitterness out of his voice. It was hard. This was turning into a lousy vacation.

Tyson shifted his weight in the chair and said, "No. The only thing I need is the story."

"Well, you know the background," Porter began. "The Agency suspected a double agent in its own house. Someone pretty high up. They told you to find the man. You put me and Carradine on it. The traitor had the code name 'Puppeteer.' That was because—from what we could piece together—he was running his own 'Agency within an Agency.' He got other American agents to go over to the KGB. Our plan was that I would set myself up as a candidate for the Puppeteer's team."

"You and Carradine were a bad combination," Tyson admitted.

"As you recall, it wasn't my idea. . . ."

Porter recounted the day he was given his assignment. He felt cold as he was telling the story. It had been winter in Washington. Whenever Porter thought of Washington, he always felt cold. He felt even colder when he remembered his meeting with Carradine.

"James, you'll be working with Tom Carradine," he remembered Tyson saying. Carradine's handshake had been hard, almost cruel. As though he were trying to prove something.

Porter never liked working with other agents. They always just seemed to get in the way. And Carradine was to prove no different.

"Let's go get this guy," Carradine told Porter after their meeting. His gung-ho manner bothered Porter from the beginning. It was as though Carradine thought he was going after an escaped convict instead of a master spy. But Porter felt he couldn't say anything. Carradine was too close to Tyson.

"The Puppeteer's going to come to us," Porter replied. "I know a man who can arrange a meeting. His name is Robertson. He's a soldier-for-hire. Knows almost everybody on *both* sides. He won't know the Puppeteer himself, but he'll get us close."

"You're going to trust a mercenary? They'd sell their own mothers—"

"Listen, Carradine. The Puppeteer isn't going to advertise. I've got to get the word out."

"So who made you the boss?" Carradine sneered.

"If you've got another idea, spill it. Otherwise, stow it," Porter said. Carradine was quiet.

"You won't have Tyson to protect you out there," Porter said. "Meet me at the Reflecting Pool, at the Washington Monument end. At midnight."

"How do you know Robertson will show?" Carradine asked.

"He'll show," Porter said.

The night he met Robertson was bitterly cold. The Reflecting Pool was frozen. Midnight came and went and there was no sign of either Robertson or Carradine.

Porter trusted Robertson. He'd dealt with him before. He could not say the same for Carradine. Porter waited in the cold, thinking of Maine and how wonderful his trip would be when this was all over.

From a small grove of cherry trees, Porter saw three quick bursts of light. It was Robertson's signal. He was waiting. Porter took a quick look around to see if Carradine was nearby. There wasn't a soul out walking. In the street some cabs prowled the area. It wasn't a night for sight-seeing.

Porter cursed Carradine beneath his breath and walked toward Robertson's light. It would have been nice to have back-up—even if it was someone like Carradine. According to instructions, Porter stopped short of the grove of trees by about ten paces. He lit a cigarette, and then dropped it and crushed it into the ground. Robertson came out of the shadows.

He was a big man, about six feet three inches tall. He wore a leather flight jacket and a wool turtleneck. He looked cold.

"I thought you said you'd have a friend," he growled.

"A no-show," Porter stated flatly.

"You'd better play straight with me, Porter," Robertson warned.

"Don't I always?" Porter slowly lifted the lapel of his overcoat, reached in, and removed a white envelope. He handed it to Robertson, who pocketed it.

"You want to count it?" asked Porter.

"If I thought I needed to count it, I wouldn't be here."

"I want to get to the Puppeteer."

"Is he that much of a problem for you boys?" Robertson asked.

"There's a leak inside the Agency big enough to sink it. The Puppeteer's our man."

"Leave it alone," Robertson said. "For your own good."

"No can do. I'm on orders."

"Those are deadly orders."

"Suppose I wanted to go over to the other side?" Porter said.

"He'd be the man to see," Robertson said.

"Can you arrange a meeting?"

"Nope. Closest I can get you is a woman named Marta."

"Marta who?"

"Just Marta to you. She might be able to help. I'll tell her you're interested in walking away from the Agency."

"How do I get in touch with her?" asked Porter.

"She'll find you."

Robertson disappeared. Porter started to walk away, back toward his car. When he reached it, he saw that Carradine was leaning against the hood of the car. He was taking a long, lazy drag on a cigarette.

"Where were you?" Porter asked, spitting out the words.

Carradine's reply was casual. "I was just watching your moves. You're pretty good."

"I don't need an audience," Porter said.

Carradine just snickered.

Wes Tyson rose and opened a window. It was getting stuffy in the cabin. A cold breeze wafted through the room. It smelled of lilacs and damp grass. Porter waited for him to speak. He wondered what the Old Man was thinking.

"You told me you wanted Carradine off the case," Tyson said finally. "So, I took him off."

"I had to go it alone. I didn't trust him. And I still don't."

"He feels the same way," Tyson said.

"So I gathered," Porter said.

"That doesn't matter anyway."

"And what does?"

"Marta," Tyson said.

Porter had known all along that Marta's name would come up again. He had hoped Tyson might hit on something else. But deep down, he knew Marta was the flaw in his story, the part that Tyson would never buy.

"What about her?" Porter asked, testing the waters.

Tyson grew angry. "Don't play stupid with me. You mention her in the report, and then drop her completely. You said she contacted you, but never showed up to meet you. That doesn't wash."

"How do you know that?" Porter asked.

"I had Carradine tail you."

"*What?*" Porter could not believe it.

"I know you saw her three times. But you only write about one meeting in your report. And I don't know what you talked about. Now you'd better come clean, son. I want to know all about Marta. Who is she? What do you know about her? And most importantly, I want to know where she is now."

Porter's feelings of guilt were only matched by his anger at having been watched. And he was confused by the way the Old Man was acting. First he comes up to the cabin without warning. Then he says he's retiring. He says he wants Porter to take his place. He claims to trust him. But he's had him watched—and by Carradine. Porter's head was spinning. But one thing was certain. Tyson meant business. Porter would have to tell all. He swallowed hard and began.

"The first time I met Marta was New Year's Eve. . . ."

It had snowed heavily in the nation's capital on Christmas Day. The snow was white and clean and had given the city the charm of a toyland town. By the new year, it had turned black and grimy.

Porter had received a large box in the mail a week before. It had been brightly wrapped in red and green paper. When he opened it, he found a small white card with an address on it. It mentioned New Year's Eve. It was signed "Marta."

Porter showed up on the appointed day and time. He paid little attention to the apartment itself. If the Puppeteer was as good as Porter thought, the meeting places would change from time to time. By the next day, there would be no trace left of either Marta or the Puppeteer.

Porter walked up a flight of stairs. The door at the top of the stairs was slightly ajar. He walked in. The place was warm. A fire was blazing. But the apartment was empty. There wasn't even a chair in the room.

Marta appeared from a back bedroom. She was tall, thin, and dressed in black. Her pale skin, set against the dark dress she wore, looked snow white. Her hair was long and black.

She stood staring at him—through him. It made Porter edgy.

Finally she said, "You're a liar." She said it simply and flatly as though she were stating his height or weight.

Porter was taken aback. "I haven't said anything yet."

"You don't need to. It's in your eyes. You're trying to trap him."

"Am I?"

"Yes. And you want me to help you do it. I won't."

"I want to defect," Porter lied.

Marta said nothing as she walked to the front door. Then she opened it, signaling Porter to leave. "Good night," she said. The way she said it left no doubt that she meant it.

Porter knew there was no point in trying another tack. He turned up his collar and walked into the night.

It was a lousy first meeting.

Porter spent the rest of the week thinking about two things: how to find another way to get to the Puppeteer, and how to see Marta again.

He didn't have to think long. Five days after his first meeting with the mysterious

Marta, he received another present. This one was also wrapped in red and green. And it was also empty except for another card signed "Marta." This time he was to meet her in front of a museum at twelve noon on Saturday.

Porter was grateful for the chance to see her again. He was also grateful that it was a warm, sunny day. The snow was melting, and the air was clean and crisp. He saw Marta sitting on a bench and tossing seed to the pigeons which had gathered at her feet. He sat down beside her.

"I know who you are," she told him.

"Oh?"

"You are James K. Porter. People call you J. K. You have been a CIA agent for 20 years. You are not married. You have no children. You work for a man named Wes

Tyson and you have no intention of defecting."

"So . . . the leak *is* very bad," Porter said.

"Yes."

"So why did you ask to see me again if you knew all this?"

Marta tossed some more feed to the pigeons. The birds began cautiously waddling back to her after having flown away when Porter sat down.

"Because . . . because I like you. I wanted to warn you not to get more involved with this case."

"It's too late for that."

"You don't know how deeply this goes. The double agent is deep within your organization. If you go on with this, you will get yourself killed, and me killed as well."

"If you're that close to the Puppeteer, then you can help."

"It is exactly *because* I am so close that I cannot help."

"The Puppeteer is a traitor."

"I know."

"I could force you to help me."

Marta smiled kindly, as to a child. "No. I am protected by both your agency and the KGB. I am perhaps as safe as the Puppeteer."

Porter looked at her. For the first time he saw how beautiful she was. A few nights ago, in the dimly lit apartment, she only looked dark and mysterious. In the sunlight, her face was softer, lighter. When she smiled, he felt weak.

"I have to go," she said.

"Can I see you again?" asked Porter.

"There's no point."

"Yes," Porter said, looking deeply into her eyes. "Yes, there is."

Porter felt there had been no need to give Wes Tyson the details about his and Marta's next meetings. They had had nothing to do with spies, or double agents, or the KGB. True, Marta's feelings for Porter had caused her to agree to arrange a meeting with the Puppeteer. And true, Porter did finally meet him—if only in the frozen shadows of the Lincoln Memorial. If only from 50 paces.

But Porter felt there was no need to explain about that last meeting. He had left it out of the report. And he saw no need to mention it now, here in Maine, talking to Tyson. Besides, the meeting had come to nothing. Afraid of what she had done, Marta had fired her weapon into the sky to frighten off both Porter *and* the Puppeteer. Then she had quickly disappeared. Porter never saw her again.

The fire was dying down. Tyson played with his empty glass, taking in all that Porter had just told him. Porter sat in silence like a schoolboy, awaiting punishment. He was hoping that his honesty—however late in coming—might spare him.

"So . . ." Tyson said, taking a deep breath, "that's it, is it?"

Porter nodded.

"You fell in love with this Marta. And she fell in love with you. And you kept her out of the report for fear someone from our side might get to her."

"Something like that," Porter said.

"That was foolish," Tyson said.

"Yes."

A loon cackled in the distance, a common sound coming from Seven Tree Lake. Tyson stirred uncomfortably at the strange sound.

"Where is she now?" asked Tyson.

"I don't know."

"I'll need to find her. Question her. She must have told you something?"

"She can't help," Porter protested. "She won't help. She said herself that she's protected by both sides. I don't know how or why."

"My bosses will never buy that," Tyson growled.

"They'll have to."

Porter rose and shoveled cold ash over the last few burning embers. It was his way of saying the conversation was over. Promotion or no promotion, that was the way it happened.

But Tyson was not about to let go.

"The woman is the key," the Old Man said. "You tell me you never saw her again?"

"That's right."

"The final meeting, at the Lincoln Memorial—she never said a word? She just fired her weapon and disappeared?"

Porter stopped burying the embers. He froze. He felt sweaty and cold at once.

"You're letting love get the better of you," Tyson added. "That's something I expect from a rookie. You're still holding back. What else do you know?"

"How did you know about the meeting at the Lincoln Memorial?" Porter asked.

"It was in your report," Tyson replied.

Porter had dropped off the report days ago. It was filled with many facts, figures, and events. It spanned months of work.

Porter had written every page of it, and knew every word. And of one thing he was certain—he never mentioned the meeting at the Lincoln Memorial. The only people who knew of that meeting were the three people who were there that night.

Porter's blood turned cold. His skin crawled. He swallowed hard and tasted something bitter in the back of his throat. "Oh. I'd forgotten," he said.

He saw Tyson smile. It was a kind, fatherly smile. "Well," the Old Man began, "I guess I've grilled you enough for one night. I'm tired."

"The Maine air will do that to you," Porter said weakly. "There's a small bedroom upstairs," he added. "You're welcome to it."

"Sounds good," Tyson yawned. He started up the stairs. Then he turned to Porter and said, "Don't worry, James. I understand about the girl. It's happened to me. I'll see what I can do for you. I'll have Carradine track her down."

Porter looked kindly at the Old Man as he walked upstairs. But his mind was racing, thinking of what to do next. "Care for another sherry before bed?" he asked.

"Why not?" said Tyson.

"I'll bring it up to you."

Tyson headed up the stairs and out of sight. Porter was glad that the Old Man could not see him shaking as he poured the sherry in the glass. Shaking as he set the glass on a tray. Shaking as he drugged Tyson's drink.

For a year, Porter had searched for the Puppeteer with no success. Now, in a small town in Maine, he was actually sharing a cabin with him.

Porter brought the drink to Tyson and set it by his bed. Tyson thanked him. Porter said something about not sleeping too late if he wanted to catch any fish. They both said good night. Porter shut the door.

He went right to work. Alex, the postman, would be coming by in a few minutes on his way home from work. Porter knew that if Tyson took the drink, he'd be out for a solid 12 hours. It would be enough time to get a message out through Alex.

Porter scribbled a note and a phone number on a piece of paper and folded it once. He addressed it to Alex. The mailbox was a good walk—down at the end of the drive—but Porter wasn't worried. Tyson's room faced away from the road and toward the lake. If Porter was quiet, Tyson would never even know he had left the house.

Upstairs, the Old Man took hold of the sherry glass and sat back in his bed. He held the glass up to his lips. He held it beneath his nose and sniffed. Then he smiled, almost proudly, admiring the man he had called his student. He rose from his bed and opened the window. He poured the sherry into the windowsill and watched the bare, rough wood soak up the liquid. He set the glass back on the tray, closed his eyes, and went to sleep.

Porter stayed awake for most of the night. An hour before dawn, however, he finally let go and fell asleep. The sun was just rising over the lake when he jerked himself awake. He swore at himself silently and shook his head. He stumbled to the sink, and threw some cold water on his face.

He had dreamt about Marta and Tyson and the meeting at the Lincoln Memorial. But now he was awake. He knew this was no dream. And he knew what to do. He'd put on a pot of coffee just in case Tyson hadn't taken the drink. Just in case he was waking up. That way, it would look like business as usual.

He looked out at the mailbox. The red flag was down. Alex had taken the message. It had gone off without a hitch.

Porter smiled. Everything was under control. If the Old Man was asleep, there would be no problem. And even if he hadn't taken the drug, all Porter would have to do was humor him for a few hours. The Agency would send help.

He checked on the coffee, then poured himself a cup. His hands were steady and calm—no shaking now. He even felt a little sadness. All the years he had spent with Tyson—it all seemed like such a waste. He took a sip of coffee and enjoyed the moment. In a few hours it would all be over. He'd have the Puppeteer, finally.

The voice which suddenly rose up from the stairwell seemed to be mocking him. "When did you find out?"

He turned to see Tyson pointing a gun at him.

Porter sighed. "Last night, when you mentioned the meeting at the Lincoln Memorial. I never put that in my report."

Tyson winced, obviously embarrassed. "Very dumb mistake on my part. Almost as bad as that drugged drink you handed me. We'll both have to try to do better."

Porter thought of a hundred different things to ask Tyson. But all he could manage was, "Why?"

"Your report was so sketchy. I was afraid you had gone over my head. Telling my bosses that I was the one, and then telling me what I wanted to hear. The next day you left for Maine, and a day later Marta vanished."

"Who is Marta to you, Wes? Who is she?"

Tyson sighed heavily and lowered his gun. For a moment, Porter thought of jumping him. But at this distance it was too risky. "Marta?" Tyson said, as in a dream. "Marta was the result of a relationship between myself and a very beautiful Russian spy."

"Marta's your *daughter*?"

Tyson nodded. Porter was shocked.

"Years ago, Irena—her mother—asked me to get some Agency names," Tyson said. "It seemed harmless enough. And it gave me a chance to see Marta. You have no idea how silly all this game-playing seems when you have a child in the middle. I would have done anything to keep Marta safe and happy. So I helped her mother once, and then I kept on helping her.

"Irena died a few years ago. But the demands for information kept coming. Soon, I was recruiting people for the KGB. By this time they knew they had me. They could serve me up to my own people anytime they wanted to for the spying I had done. And I knew Marta would be safe only if I continued to help them...."

Tyson's voice trailed off, and tears welled in his eyes. Porter studied him closely, watching the trigger finger. It did not ease up. His aim remained true. Tyson went on, his voice cracking from time to time. Slowly his sorrow eased and his anger increased. "But all these years she's lived like a gypsy— on the run. She's had every chance to expose me. But she never did...."

"Except for the night at the Lincoln Memorial," said Porter.

Tyson nodded. "Yes. She told me I was to meet a KGB agent. She said that the KGB was willing to end the blackmail if I did one more job. You were in the shadows. But I didn't know it was you. I just walked toward you...." Now the gun shook slightly.

"But she stopped you by firing her gun above our heads." Porter said calmly. "She couldn't go through with it."

"She always loved me. Even though I could never love her fully, not like a father should."

Tyson lowered his gun, its barrel aimed toward the floor. Porter knew that if he were going to make a move, he'd have to do it now. If he jumped at Tyson, he'd give him just enough time to raise his gun. Porter would surely be wounded, but the chances were good he would not be killed. Tyson was too upset to react quickly or clearly.

Then Porter spied another option. The coffee. He grabbed the pot and flung the contents at Tyson.

The coffee spattered onto Tyson, who cried out in pain. His gun exploded, once shattering a window, then again splintering the table, and a third time knocking a lamp over. Porter could not get near the man. He didn't know how many more times Tyson would fire. But he knew Tyson would soon recover from the shock and hit his mark.

Porter ran.

He headed for the woods. He figured he'd have the best chance there. Tyson might have the weapons and the firepower. But Porter was younger, stronger, and knew the woods well. His only weapon was a pocket knife.

Porter entered the woods as fast as he could. Tyson was not far behind. Porter looked back only once to see Tyson take aim. Porter threw himself into a ditch just as Tyson fired. A branch, shattered by the bullet, fell, and landed a foot away from him. He rolled over and scrambled for the safety of a thick grove of trees.

Tyson, seeing Porter disappear into the woods, calmed down. He had Porter on the run. He drew a second gun from his coat and clutched it tightly in his left hand. He moved into the woods, listening for the slightest sound.

Porter darted quickly through the woods like a rabbit—swift, quiet, sure.

The first thing he knew he had to do was make himself a weapon. The pocket knife was a sad form of defense, although it would do the trick up close. What Porter needed was a long-range weapon. He scooped up a straight stick, heavy, but still moist. On a calmer, more peaceful day, it might make a good walking stick. Today it would have to serve as a spear.

As he ran, Porter started chopping away at the end, sharpening it. But to make a truly deadly point, he would have to find a place to hide and work. He headed for a bluff high above the pine trees.

When he reached the bluff, Porter found a small group of bushes and low trees. From here, he could see most of the woods and not be seen himself. As he worked, he stole quick glances down at the woods. There was no sign of Tyson.

The hairs on Porter's head bristled. He should be able to see some sign of the man. "Think, Porter, think," he told himself. "Where did he go? What is he doing?"

Perhaps it was the feeling of being watched. Or it may have been the gentle sound of a cracking twig. But something made Porter turn. And there, above him, not 50 feet away, he saw Wes Tyson, stalking him quietly.

In the thick, summer greens of the woods, the Old Man had not yet spotted

Porter. But Porter knew that the slightest sound would give away his position. If he tried to use his spear, the cracking of the branches and dead leaves beneath him would give him away. And his spear was no match in either speed or accuracy for the bullets that Tyson would fire at him.

Tyson spotted Porter just as he stood to get in position to throw his spear. Tyson fired. Porter felt a stinging in his hand. Then it went numb. He realized that Tyson's shot had split the spear, splintering the point into a jagged mess. Porter dropped the stick and jumped for cover, landing with a thud. Tyson fired once more and missed. The sound of gunshots echoed through the woods.

Porter twisted his ankle in the fall and continued to tumble down the hill. He skidded through thorny bushes and wild branches. The prickly weeds tore at his flesh and ripped his clothes. The woods seemed to be spinning around him, a blur of yellow, green, and gold. He tried to regain his balance, but he was dropping too fast.

He rolled onto an open path. Before he could even think about trying to stand, Porter felt the barrel of a gun pressed up against his skull. "Don't move," he heard the man growl. "And don't make a sound."

Porter looked up into the angry face of Tom Carradine.

Wes Tyson heard the cry of a man. Someone was calling for him. He cautiously cocked the triggers of both his weapons and moved down the hill. If

Porter had survived his fall, he would only have his wits to save him now. Tyson knew Porter would try any trick to save himself. He walked off the path and doubled back, moving behind the sound of the voice.

Then Tyson saw him. He could not believe it at first. Porter was on his hands and knees. Above him, clutching a rifle and pointing it at Porter's temple, was Carradine.

"Wes!" Carradine called. "Wes, I got your man."

Tyson moved out of the woods and onto the path.

Carradine smiled at him. "That woman Porter had been contacting waltzed into the Agency yesterday."

"Marta?" Tyson tried to hide his surprise and concern.

"That's the one," Carradine said. "She told us that our friend Porter, here, had been using her to recruit double agents. Wes, you're looking at the Puppeteer himself—J. K. Porter."

"You don't know what you're talking about—" Porter said.

"Shut up, traitor," Carradine said, cutting him off.

"Good work, Carradine," Tyson said. He put both his weapons away. "I'll need to see the woman as soon as possible," he added.

As soon as Tyson had stowed his weapons, Carradine eased the gun away from Porter. And he pointed it right at the Old Man's chest. "Sorry, Wes. Please don't move, or I'll have to shoot you. Can you get his guns, Porter?"

"I think so," Porter said and hobbled toward Tyson. Porter stripped him of both weapons. As he did, the Old Man stood in silence, stunned.

"We got a distress message from Porter," Carradine explained. "He said he'd found the Puppeteer."

"What?" bellowed Tyson. "You're going to believe this man? What about Marta? What about what she told you. *Porter's* the traitor!"

"She *did* walk into the Agency," Carradine stated coldly. "And she did tell us everything, Wes. Everything."

Wes Tyson saw the look on Carradine's face. He realized that Carradine did, in fact, know the truth. "I guess she just got tired of running," Tyson said. He smiled once more. "Then it's finally all over," he said weakly. "All the years of lies and hiding. It's all over."

"Let's go, Wes," Porter said.

"Can I see Marta?" Tyson asked. "Can I at least see my daughter?"

"Sure," Carradine replied. "Sure."

Porter and Carradine signaled Tyson to put his hands on his head and walk several paces in front of them. In a daze, Tyson obeyed.

When he was just out of earshot, Porter asked. "How is Marta?"

Carradine shook his head. "We turned our backs on her for less than a minute, Porter. But she was very upset. It was a cyanide pill. When we turned around she was already dying. She said to say goodbye to you."

Porter stopped in his tracks and told Carradine to move on ahead. He watched as both men walked out of sight. Suddenly the Maine woods were quiet once more.

Porter found an old tree stump and sat. His ankle was throbbing, but he didn't much care. He was just tired. He thought of Marta until it hurt too much. He tried to convince himself that he would never go back to Washington again. He sighed deeply, and looked up toward the sky. "Some vacation," he moaned.

He heard a loon out on the lake laughing at him. He heard birds chirping in the trees above him. He breathed in the heavy smell of the pines. All the horrors of the past 24 hours slowly began to fade.

He found a stick, tall, straight, and sturdy. He grabbed it and used it as a crutch. He walked down a path away from Carradine and Tyson. Toward the lake. "Maybe," he thought, "I can still get some fishing in."